My Neighbor is an Inventor: A Journey into Wilson's World of Innovation

Step into the extraordinary realm of Wilson, your neighbor and the genius inventor behind a series of groundbreaking creations that are reshaping our world. In the captivating pages of "My Neighbor is an Inventor," each chapter unveils a new marvel:

Witness the ingenuity of Wilson and His Self-Trimming Hedges, where automated sensors ensure pristine landscapes year-round. Experience Wilson's Solar-Powered Lawn Mower, silently revolutionizing lawn care with renewable energy. Delve into Wilson's Weather-Controlled Planters, pioneering sustainable agriculture with automated climate adjustments.

Follow the evolution of Wilson's Personal Drone Courier System, transforming logistics with efficient and eco-friendly delivery solutions. Embark on an adventure with Wilson's Virtual Reality Portal Pod, transporting users to fantastical realms for immersive experiences in artifact collecting.

Meet Wilson and His Robotic Pet Companion, a lifelike marvel offering companionship with emotional intelligence. Explore Wilson's Robotic Rainwater

Collection Hydroponic Garden, a fusion of water conservation and urban agriculture.

Discover Wilson's Smart Trash Compactor, heralding a cleaner future with automated waste management. And ensure peace of mind with Wilson's Augmented Reality Home Security System, merging cutting-edge technology with home protection.

"My Neighbor is an Inventor" is more than a collection of inventions; it's a testament to Wilson's passion for innovation and his commitment to enhancing our lives. Whether you're captivated by advanced technology or fascinated by the possibilities of the future, Wilson's creations will inspire, educate, and ignite your imagination. Join us on this journey into the mind of Maplewood's inventive genius and envision a world transformed by ingenuity and creativity.

The Genius Next Door: Wilson and His Self-Trimming Hedges

Living in the quaint suburban neighborhood of Willowbrook, I often marveled at the picturesque lawns, each home seemingly vying for the title of "Yard of the Month." But there was one yard that always stood out, not because of its competition for the title but because it never needed to. The home belonged to my incredibly intelligent neighbor, Wilson.

Wilson was the kind of neighbor everyone wished they had. He was always willing to lend a hand, share a cup of sugar, or offer a piece of sage advice. But more than anything, he was known for his brilliant inventions. A retired engineer with a penchant for tinkering, Wilson's garage was a treasure trove of gadgets and gizmos that seemed straight out of a science fiction novel.

One sunny Saturday morning, I noticed Wilson in his front yard, meticulously adjusting something on his latest creation. Curiosity piqued, I walked over to see what he was up to.

"Morning, Wilson! What have you got there?" I asked, peering over the fence.

"Good morning! I'm glad you asked," Wilson replied with a twinkle in his eye. "I'm working on my newest invention— Self-Trimming Hedges."

I raised an eyebrow. "Self-Trimming Hedges? How do they work?"

Wilson wiped his hands on a rag and motioned for me to come closer. "Let me show you," he said, leading me to a row of impeccably trimmed hedges lining his driveway. "These hedges are equipped with sensors that detect growth. When the sensors register that the hedges have grown beyond a certain point, tiny, integrated blades trim them back to the perfect shape and height."

As he explained, Wilson pointed to a small, barely noticeable device embedded within the foliage. "The system is powered by solar energy and designed to be as unobtrusive as possible. The sensors are incredibly precise, ensuring the hedges remain in optimal condition year-round."

I was amazed. "That's incredible, Wilson! How did you come up with the idea?"

Wilson smiled. "It all started when I noticed how much time and effort my neighbors, especially the elderly ones, spent maintaining their yards. I wanted to create something that would make their lives easier while keeping our neighborhood looking beautiful."

I watched in fascination as Wilson demonstrated the system. He used a remote control to simulate hedge growth, and within seconds, the tiny blades whirred to life, trimming the excess foliage with surgical precision. The result was a perfectly manicured hedge that looked as if it had just been tended to by a professional landscaper.

"That's amazing," I said, genuinely impressed. "Have you tested it in different weather conditions?"

Wilson nodded. "Absolutely. I've designed the system to withstand various weather conditions. The sensors are waterproof, and the blades are made from a special alloy that resists rust and corrosion. I've also implemented a safety mechanism that stops the blades if they encounter anything other than foliage, so it's safe for pets and children."

As word of Wilson's Self-Trimming Hedges spread, neighbors began to gather in his front yard, eager to see the invention in action. Wilson, always the gracious host, was more than happy to explain the intricacies of his creation to anyone who asked.

Over the next few weeks, Wilson's invention became the talk of the neighborhood. People were fascinated by the idea of hedges that maintained themselves, and many expressed interest in having the system installed in their own yards. Wilson, ever the altruist, decided to offer his invention at cost to his neighbors, wanting to share the benefits of his creation without seeking profit.

One evening, as we sat on Wilson's porch enjoying a cold drink, he confided in me. "You know, I've always believed that inventions should serve a greater purpose. It's not just about creating

something new; it's about making
people's lives better."

His words resonated with me. Wilson's
Self-Trimming Hedges were more than
just a clever invention; they were a
testament to his kindness and ingenuity.
He had found a way to use his talents to
improve the lives of those around him,
and in doing so, he had brought the
community closer together.

As the months went by, the
neighborhood underwent a
transformation. The once time-
consuming task of hedge trimming
became a thing of the past, freeing up
residents to spend more time with their

families and pursue their passions. The perfectly manicured hedges added to the charm of Willowbrook, making it an even more delightful place to live.

Wilson's invention also sparked a wave of creativity among the younger generation. Inspired by his ingenuity, local kids began to explore their own ideas and inventions, often seeking Wilson's guidance. He became a mentor to many, encouraging them to think outside the box and follow their dreams.

One such young inventor was Sarah, a bright and curious teenager who lived a few houses down. She had always been fascinated by technology and often visited Wilson's garage to ask questions and seek advice. With Wilson's encouragement, Sarah developed her own invention—a smart irrigation system that adjusted water usage based on weather forecasts and soil moisture levels. Like Wilson's Self-Trimming Hedges, Sarah's system helped conserve resources and made life easier for the community.

Wilson's influence extended beyond our neighborhood. News of his Self-Trimming Hedges caught the attention of a local news station, and soon his story was broadcast across the city. People from all over began to reach out, wanting to learn more about his invention and how they could implement similar systems in their own communities.

Despite the growing recognition, Wilson remained humble. "I'm just glad to be able to help," he would say whenever someone praised his work. "If my invention can make a difference, then that's all the reward I need."

One day, while walking past Wilson's house, I noticed a group of city officials gathered in his yard. Curious, I approached and discovered that they were there to discuss the possibility of implementing Wilson's Self-Trimming Hedges in public parks and green spaces throughout the city. The idea of having perfectly maintained hedges in public areas without the need for constant upkeep was an appealing prospect, and Wilson was more than happy to assist in making it a reality.

As I watched Wilson explain his invention to the officials, I couldn't help but feel a sense of pride. Here was my neighbor, using his brilliance to make the world a better place, one hedge at a time.

In the years that followed, Wilson's Self-Trimming Hedges became a common sight not just in Willowbrook but in neighborhoods and public spaces across the region. His invention had revolutionized the way people approached yard maintenance, freeing them from a tedious chore and allowing them to enjoy their surroundings to the fullest.

Wilson continued to invent, always looking for ways to solve everyday problems with his unique blend of creativity and technical expertise. His garage remained a hub of activity, a place where ideas were born and nurtured.

But for all his inventions and accolades, Wilson never lost sight of what mattered most: community. He remained the same kind, generous neighbor who was always ready to lend a hand or share a word of wisdom. His Self-Trimming Hedges were a testament to his ingenuity, but his true legacy was the sense of togetherness and inspiration he brought to Willowbrook.

As I sit on my porch, looking out at the perfectly trimmed hedges lining the street, I can't help but smile. Wilson's invention may have changed our neighborhood's landscape, but it was his spirit of innovation and community that truly transformed our lives. And for that, we would always be grateful.

The Silent Revolution: Wilson and His Solar-Powered Lawn Mower

Life in Maplewood was the picture of suburban tranquility, where weekends were dedicated to barbecues, children played in the streets, and neighbors chatted over white picket fences. Amidst this idyllic backdrop, one house stood out—not for its extravagance, but for the ingenious mind that resided within. My incredibly intelligent neighbor, Wilson, was known far and wide for his remarkable inventions. A retired engineer with a penchant for solving everyday problems through innovation,

Wilson's home was a veritable laboratory of ideas, with his garage as the heart of his creative endeavors.

It was early spring when Wilson unveiled his latest creation. As the first hints of green began to emerge in lawns around the neighborhood, so did the familiar roar of lawn mowers, a sound that punctuated the weekends with its persistent buzz. But on this particular Saturday morning, the usual cacophony was absent. Curious, I strolled over to Wilson's yard, where I found him standing next to a sleek, futuristic-looking device.

"Morning, Wilson," I greeted him. "What have you cooked up this time?"

Wilson beamed with the enthusiasm of a child showing off a prized toy. "Good morning! Meet my newest invention— the Solar-Powered Lawn Mower."

The machine, about the size of a large suitcase, gleamed under the morning sun. Its smooth, aerodynamic design hinted at the advanced technology within. "How does it work?" I asked, already knowing the answer would be something extraordinary.

"Let me give you a demonstration," Wilson said, activating the mower with a small remote control. The machine hummed to life, moving silently across the grass. "It's entirely solar-powered, operating silently and autonomously. It navigates the yard using a combination of GPS and sensors, ensuring it covers every inch of the lawn. When its battery runs low, it automatically returns to a charging station to recharge."

As I watched the mower glide effortlessly over the grass, I was struck by its precision and efficiency. It neatly trimmed the blades to a uniform height, leaving behind a perfectly manicured lawn. "That's incredible, Wilson! How did you come up with the idea?"

Wilson chuckled. "I was tired of the noise and hassle of traditional lawn mowers. Plus, I wanted to create something environmentally friendly. Solar power was the obvious choice, and I knew if I could design it to be autonomous, it would save people a lot of time and effort."

Word of Wilson's Solar-Powered Lawn Mower spread quickly. By midday, a small crowd had gathered in his yard, neighbors eager to witness the silent marvel in action. Wilson, ever the gracious host, explained the features of his invention, demonstrating its capabilities and answering questions with the patience of a seasoned teacher.

Over the following weeks, the mower became the talk of Maplewood. People were fascinated by the idea of a lawn mower that operated silently and autonomously, powered entirely by the sun. Many of Wilson's neighbors expressed interest in acquiring one for themselves, and Wilson, in his usual generous fashion, offered to help them install and set up the systems in their own yards.

One evening, as we sat on Wilson's porch enjoying the warm spring air, he shared more about his motivations. "You know, it's not just about creating something new," he said thoughtfully.

"It's about making a positive impact. The Solar-Powered Lawn Mower reduces noise pollution, cuts down on fossil fuel consumption, and gives people back their time. That's what really matters."

His words resonated with me. Wilson's invention was more than just a clever gadget; it was a testament to his desire to improve the world around him. He had found a way to combine his technical expertise with his passion for sustainability, creating something that benefited both people and the planet.

As summer approached, the impact of Wilson's invention became increasingly evident. The once noisy weekend mornings were now filled with the sounds of nature—birds chirping, leaves rustling in the breeze. Neighbors who had adopted the solar-powered mowers found themselves with more free time to enjoy their weekends, no longer burdened by the chore of mowing the lawn.

Wilson's invention also inspired a sense of community. Those who had benefited from his generosity were eager to pay it forward, helping others install and maintain their own solar-powered mowers. It wasn't long before the entire neighborhood was abuzz with excitement about the possibilities of solar power and sustainable living.

One day, a representative from the local news station visited Maplewood to do a feature on Wilson's invention. As cameras rolled and reporters interviewed residents, Wilson remained humble, deflecting praise and focusing instead on the collective benefits of his creation.

"It's not about me," he told the reporter. "It's about what we can achieve together. If we all make small changes, like using solar power, we can have a big impact on our environment and our quality of life."

The news segment aired later that week, showcasing Maplewood's transformation and highlighting Wilson's role in it. People from neighboring communities reached out, eager to learn more about the Solar-Powered Lawn Mower and how they could implement similar solutions in their own neighborhoods.

Despite the growing recognition, Wilson remained the same down-to-earth neighbor we all knew and admired. He continued to tinker in his garage, always looking for new ways to solve everyday problems and make life a little better for those around him.

One summer afternoon, as I was enjoying a quiet moment in my backyard, Wilson came over with a thoughtful expression on his face. "I've been thinking," he said, taking a seat next to me. "There's so much more we can do with solar power. What if we could create a whole suite of solar-powered household devices?"

Intrigued, I listened as Wilson outlined his ideas—solar-powered leaf blowers, garden lights, even a solar-powered sprinkler system that adjusted water usage based on weather conditions. Each concept was designed with the same principles of sustainability, efficiency, and user-friendliness that had made the lawn mower such a success.

"I think it's a fantastic idea," I told him. "And I'm sure our neighbors would be eager to help you test and develop these new inventions."

Wilson's eyes sparkled with enthusiasm. "That's exactly what I was hoping you'd say. With everyone's input and support, we can turn Maplewood into a model of sustainable living."

As the weeks turned into months, Wilson's vision began to take shape. With the help of our neighbors, he developed and tested a range of solar-powered devices, each one designed to make life easier and more environmentally friendly. The garden lights illuminated our streets with a soft, energy-efficient glow, while the sprinkler system ensured our lawns remained lush and green without wasting water.

The transformation was remarkable. Maplewood became a beacon of innovation and sustainability, a community where neighbors worked together to create a better future. And at the heart of it all was Wilson, whose brilliance and generosity had sparked a silent revolution.

Looking back, it's clear that Wilson's Solar-Powered Lawn Mower was just the beginning. His invention not only improved our lives but also inspired us to think differently about the way we use and conserve energy. It brought us closer together, united by a shared commitment to sustainability and a deep appreciation for the quiet, green beauty of our surroundings.

As I sit on my porch, watching the sun set over the neatly trimmed lawns of Maplewood, I can't help but feel a profound sense of gratitude. Wilson's inventions have changed our neighborhood, but more importantly, they've changed the way we see the world. And for that, we will always be thankful.

OP

Life in Maplewood was a serene blend of suburban charm and close-knit community spirit. Neighbors often gathered for barbecues, children played in the tree-lined streets, and front yards boasted meticulously maintained gardens. Amidst this picturesque setting lived Wilson, an incredibly intelligent inventor whose innovations had a transformative effect on our neighborhood.

Wilson was a retired engineer with an insatiable curiosity and a passion for solving everyday problems. His garage was a wonderland of gadgets and prototypes, each one a testament to his creativity and technical prowess. Over the years, Wilson had introduced several remarkable inventions that had not only improved our lives but also brought us closer together as a community.

One crisp autumn morning, I noticed Wilson in his front yard, carefully arranging a series of sleek, futuristic-looking planters. Intrigued, I wandered over to see what he was up to.

"Good morning, Wilson! What's the latest creation?" I asked, peering at the planters with curiosity.

"Ah, good morning!" Wilson replied, his eyes twinkling with excitement. "I'm glad you asked. These are my newest invention—Weather-Controlled Planters."

The planters, made from a smooth, durable material, were equipped with a variety of sensors and tiny mechanisms. They looked like something out of a science fiction movie, promising an array of unseen capabilities.

"Weather-Controlled Planters? How do they work?" I inquired, eager to learn more.

"These planters are designed to optimize plant growth by monitoring and adjusting to the environmental conditions," Wilson explained. "They have sensors that measure soil moisture, sunlight, and temperature. Based on the data they collect, the planters can automatically water the plants, adjust their position to maximize sunlight, and even regulate the soil temperature to ensure optimal growth."

He bent down and tapped a few buttons on one of the planters, showing me the interface on a small, integrated screen. "For example, if the soil is too dry, the planter will automatically dispense water. If the temperature drops too low, it can activate a heating element to keep the roots warm. And if the plants need more sunlight, the planter can rotate to face the sun."

I was amazed. "That's incredible, Wilson! How did you come up with the idea?"

Wilson smiled. "I've always loved gardening, but I noticed that many people in our neighborhood struggled to keep their plants healthy, especially during extreme weather conditions. I wanted to create something that would make gardening easier and more efficient, so that everyone could enjoy the beauty and satisfaction of growing their own plants."

As Wilson demonstrated the various features of the planters, a few neighbors gathered around, drawn by the novelty of his latest invention. He explained the technology with the patience of a seasoned teacher, answering questions and showcasing the planters' capabilities.

Word of Wilson's Weather-Controlled Planters spread quickly. By the end of the week, nearly everyone in

Maplewood had heard about the revolutionary devices. Many of our neighbors, especially those with less green thumbs, were eager to get their hands on one.

Over the next few months, Wilson's invention began to take root in our community, quite literally. The planters were a hit, and soon, they were adorning front yards, backyards, and even windowsills throughout Maplewood. The once challenging task of maintaining a garden became effortless, and the results were spectacular. Lush, vibrant plants flourished in every corner of the neighborhood, creating a tapestry of colors and scents that delighted the senses.

One evening, as I sat on Wilson's porch enjoying the pleasant autumn breeze, he shared more about his motivations. "You know, gardening is more than just a hobby for me," he said thoughtfully. "It's a way to connect with nature and find peace. I wanted to make that experience accessible to everyone, regardless of their gardening skills or the climate they live in."

His words resonated with me. Wilson's Weather-Controlled Planters were more than just a clever invention; they were a gift to the community, a way to bring people closer to nature and to each other. By eliminating the barriers to successful gardening, Wilson had opened up a world of possibilities for all of us.

As winter approached, the true value of Wilson's planters became even more apparent. While the cold weather would typically spell the end of the gardening season, the Weather-Controlled Planters continued to thrive. Their built-in heating elements protected the plants from frost, and the automated watering system ensured they received the perfect amount of moisture.

Maplewood remained a green oasis amidst the stark winter landscape, and the sight of flourishing plants brought joy and a sense of continuity to our lives. The planters also sparked a wave of creativity among our neighbors, who began experimenting with different types of plants and sharing their successes and tips with one another.

One such neighbor was Mrs. Jenkins, an elderly woman who had always loved gardening but found it increasingly difficult to manage due to her age. With the help of Wilson's planters, she was able to rekindle her passion, growing a stunning array of flowers and herbs that became the envy of the neighborhood.

Mrs. Jenkins often invited us over for tea, proudly showing off her garden and sharing stories of her favorite plants.

Wilson's invention also had a profound impact on the younger generation. Inspired by the possibilities of the planters, local children and teenagers began to take an interest in gardening and environmental science. Wilson, always eager to encourage young minds, started a community gardening club, where he taught the kids about plant biology, sustainability, and the importance of caring for the environment.

One of the club's star pupils was Emily, a bright and inquisitive twelve-year-old who lived down the street. Under Wilson's guidance, Emily developed a deep love for gardening and science. She even came up with her own innovative ideas, like integrating a weather forecasting system into the planters to anticipate and adjust for upcoming changes in the weather.

As the club grew, so did the sense of community in Maplewood. Neighbors who had previously been strangers became friends, united by their shared love of gardening and their appreciation for Wilson's invention. We organized garden tours, held plant exchanges, and even started a community garden, where everyone could contribute and benefit from the collective effort.

One spring afternoon, as I was tending to my own Weather-Controlled Planters, Wilson stopped by with a thoughtful expression on his face. "I've been thinking," he said, "there's so much more we can do with this technology. What if we could create a network of interconnected planters that could communicate with each other and share data?"

Intrigued, I listened as Wilson outlined his vision. By linking the planters together, we could create a smart gardening ecosystem that would optimize plant growth on a larger scale. The planters could share information about soil conditions, sunlight, and temperature, allowing them to work together to create the best possible environment for all the plants.

"I think it's a fantastic idea," I told him. "And I'm sure our neighbors would be eager to help you test and develop this new system."

Wilson's eyes sparkled with enthusiasm. "That's exactly what I was hoping you'd say. With everyone's input and support, we can take this to the next level."

As the weeks turned into months, Wilson's vision began to take shape. With the help of our neighbors, he developed and tested the interconnected planter system, which quickly proved to be a game-changer. The networked planters worked together seamlessly, optimizing conditions and ensuring that every plant received the care it needed.

The results were astounding. Maplewood's gardens flourished like never before, with vibrant flowers, healthy vegetables, and lush greenery adorning every yard. The interconnected system also made it easier for us to share resources and knowledge, creating a truly collaborative gardening community.

Looking back, it's clear that Wilson's Weather-Controlled Planters were just the beginning. His invention not only transformed our gardens but also brought us closer together as a community. It inspired us to think creatively about how we can use technology to live more sustainably and harmoniously with nature.

As I sit on my porch, watching the sun set over the thriving gardens of Maplewood, I can't help but feel a profound sense of gratitude. Wilson's inventions have changed our neighborhood, but more importantly, they've changed the way we see the world. And for that, we will always be thankful.

Sky Couriers: Wilson and His Personal Drone Courier System

Life in the suburban haven of Maplewood was a blend of modern convenience and timeless charm. Neighbors exchanged pleasantries over neatly trimmed hedges, children played on tree-lined streets, and weekend gatherings filled the air with laughter and the aroma of barbecue. Amidst this idyllic setting, one house stood out—not for its grandeur, but for the brilliant mind that resided within. My incredibly intelligent neighbor, Wilson, was a retired engineer whose inventive genius had transformed our community more than once.

Wilson's garage was a hub of creativity, brimming with gadgets and prototypes that hinted at his endless curiosity and problem-solving prowess. His previous inventions, like the Solar-Powered Lawn Mower and Weather-Controlled Planters, had already revolutionized life in Maplewood, making it greener and more efficient. But as summer gave way to autumn, Wilson had something new up his sleeve.

One crisp morning, as I was sipping coffee on my porch, I noticed Wilson tinkering with a small, sleek device that looked like a futuristic toy helicopter. Intrigued, I walked over to see what he was working on.

"Morning, Wilson. What's the latest invention?" I asked, peering at the drone-like object in his hands.

"Good morning! You're just in time to see the debut of my newest creation— the Personal Drone Courier System,"

Wilson replied, his eyes sparkling with excitement.

"Drone Courier System?" I echoed, curiosity piqued.

Wilson grinned and motioned for me to follow him. He led me to his driveway, where several drones, each about the size of a large shoebox, were lined up neatly. "These drones are designed to deliver packages or groceries locally. They can navigate autonomously, using GPS and a suite of sensors to avoid obstacles and ensure precise deliveries. Plus, they're powered by electricity, so they reduce carbon emissions compared to traditional delivery vehicles."

As he spoke, Wilson picked up a small package and placed it in a compartment on one of the drones. With a few taps on his tablet, the drone hummed to life, lifted off the ground, and soared gracefully into the sky.

"That's incredible, Wilson! How do they work?" I asked, watching the drone as it hovered above us.

"The system is quite sophisticated," Wilson explained. "The drones are programmed with a map of the local area and can navigate to any address within a certain range. They use GPS for navigation and are equipped with cameras and sensors to detect and avoid obstacles, ensuring safe and accurate deliveries. Once they reach their destination, they can either drop off the package at a designated spot or lower it gently to the ground."

I was fascinated. "What inspired you to create this?"

Wilson smiled. "I noticed how many delivery trucks come through our neighborhood each day, contributing to traffic and pollution. I wanted to find a more efficient and environmentally friendly way to handle local deliveries.

Plus, I thought it would be pretty cool to have our own personal courier drones."

As Wilson continued to demonstrate the drones' capabilities, neighbors began to gather, drawn by the sight of the flying devices and the promise of a new convenience. Wilson explained how the drones could be used to deliver groceries, medication, or even small packages, saving time and reducing the carbon footprint of delivery services.

The reaction was overwhelmingly positive. People were excited about the idea of receiving their packages and groceries via drone, and many were eager to see the system in action.

Wilson, always generous with his inventions, offered to set up a pilot program for the neighborhood to test the drones and provide feedback.

Over the next few weeks, Wilson's drones became a common sight in Maplewood. The pilot program was a resounding success, with neighbors marveling at the efficiency and convenience of the drone deliveries. Instead of waiting for a delivery truck or making a trip to the store, they could simply place an order and have it delivered to their doorstep within minutes.

One evening, as we sat on Wilson's porch watching the sunset, he shared more about the development process. "The biggest challenge was ensuring the drones could navigate safely and accurately. I had to design a robust obstacle avoidance system and fine-tune the navigation algorithms. But seeing how much people are enjoying the service makes it all worth it."

His words resonated with me. Wilson's Personal Drone Courier System was more than just a technological marvel; it was a testament to his desire to improve our quality of life and protect the environment. By reducing the need for delivery trucks and making local deliveries more efficient, he had found a way to make a positive impact on our community and beyond.

As the pilot program continued, the benefits of Wilson's drones became increasingly evident. Traffic in Maplewood decreased, and the air seemed fresher without the constant stream of delivery trucks. People appreciated the convenience of quick, contactless deliveries, especially during busy times or bad weather. The drones also provided a lifeline for elderly or immobile residents, who could now receive essential items without leaving their homes.

Wilson's invention also sparked a wave of enthusiasm among the younger generation. Kids and teenagers were fascinated by the drones, and Wilson, ever the educator, took the time to explain the technology and principles behind them. He started a drone club, where he taught the basics of drone operation, programming, and maintenance, inspiring a new generation of budding inventors.

One of the club's standout members was Jake, a bright and inquisitive fifteen-year-old who lived a few houses down. Under Wilson's guidance, Jake developed his own modifications for the drones, such as improved battery life and more efficient delivery algorithms. His passion for drones soon spread to his friends, and the club became a hotspot of creativity and innovation.

As the months passed, Wilson's Personal Drone Courier System caught the attention of local businesses. Small shops and restaurants saw the potential for using drones to deliver their products more efficiently. Wilson collaborated with them to integrate the drones into their delivery services, providing a boost to the local economy and reducing their environmental impact.

The success of Wilson's drones also attracted media attention. A local news station featured a story on Maplewood's drone revolution, highlighting the positive changes brought about by Wilson's invention. Interviews with residents showcased their appreciation for the convenience and environmental benefits of the drones.

Despite the growing recognition, Wilson remained humble and focused on his mission. "It's not about the fame," he would say. "It's about making a difference. If my invention can help reduce our carbon footprint and improve people's lives, then that's all the reward I need."

One spring afternoon, as I was enjoying a quiet moment in my backyard, Wilson stopped by with a thoughtful expression on his face. "I've been thinking," he said, "there's still so much we can do with drone technology. What if we could expand the system to cover larger areas and support more complex deliveries?"

Intrigued, I listened as Wilson outlined his vision. By upgrading the drones with longer battery life and more advanced navigation systems, we could extend their range and capabilities. He also proposed developing specialized drones for different types of deliveries, such as temperature-controlled drones for transporting perishable items or larger drones for bulkier packages.

"I think it's a fantastic idea," I told him. "And I'm sure our neighbors and local businesses would be eager to support the expansion."

Wilson's eyes sparkled with enthusiasm. "That's exactly what I was hoping you'd say. With everyone's input and support, we can take this to the next level."

As the weeks turned into months, Wilson's vision began to take shape. With the help of our neighbors and local businesses, he developed and tested the upgraded drone system. The new drones could cover larger areas, handle more complex deliveries, and even coordinate with each other to optimize routes and reduce energy consumption.

The results were astounding. Maplewood's skies were soon filled with a fleet of efficient, environmentally friendly drones, seamlessly delivering packages and groceries to residents and businesses. The expanded system brought even greater convenience and environmental benefits, further solidifying Maplewood's reputation as a model of innovation and sustainability.

Looking back, it's clear that Wilson's Personal Drone Courier System was more than just an invention; it was a catalyst for change. His drones not only transformed the way we received deliveries but also inspired us to think creatively about how technology can improve our lives and protect our planet.

As I sit on my porch, watching the drones flit gracefully through the evening sky, I can't help but feel a profound sense of gratitude. Wilson's inventions have changed our neighborhood, but more importantly, they've changed the way we see the world. And for that, we will always be thankful.

Beyond Reality: Wilson and His Virtual Reality Portal Pod

Life in Maplewood was a harmonious blend of suburban comfort and community spirit, where neighbors were friends and every weekend promised gatherings filled with laughter. Among these friends was Wilson, an incredibly intelligent inventor whose remarkable creations had transformed our lives more than once. His home, modest yet intriguing, housed a garage that was a testament to his inventive mind. Over the years, Wilson had introduced several groundbreaking inventions, each designed to solve everyday problems and enrich our community.

One brisk autumn morning, I noticed Wilson in his driveway, assembling what appeared to be a large, futuristic-looking pod. Intrigued, I walked over to see what he was working on.

"Good morning, Wilson! What's the latest invention?" I asked, eyeing the sleek, metallic structure with curiosity.

"Morning! I'm glad you asked," Wilson replied, his face lighting up with excitement. "This is my newest creation—the Virtual Reality Portal Pod."

"Virtual Reality Portal Pod?" I echoed, fascinated. "What does it do?"

Wilson grinned and motioned for me to step closer. "It's a portal to another world, quite literally. The pod is equipped with immersive virtual reality technology that transports users to tranquil environments for unique adventures, like alien artifact collecting. It's designed to provide a fully immersive experience, allowing you to explore and interact with these virtual worlds as if you were really there."

As he spoke, Wilson opened the pod's door, revealing a comfortable seat surrounded by high-tech screens and sensors. He invited me to take a seat, and I eagerly obliged, excited to experience his latest invention firsthand.

"Alright, let's get you started," Wilson said, securing a lightweight VR headset over my eyes. The screens lit up, and within moments, I found myself standing on an alien landscape, bathed in the soft glow of a distant sun. Strange, beautiful flora surrounded me, and the air was filled with the gentle hum of unseen creatures.

"This is amazing!" I exclaimed, turning my head to take in the breathtaking scenery. "It feels so real!"

Wilson's voice came through the headset, guiding me. "You're now on the planet Xerion, a tranquil world known for its rare and valuable artifacts. Use the handheld controller to move around and interact with the environment. Your mission is to collect as many artifacts as you can find."

I followed Wilson's instructions, marveling at the seamless realism of the experience. Every step felt natural, every object tangible. As I explored the alien landscape, I stumbled upon glowing crystals, ancient relics, and mysterious devices, each one more fascinating than the last.

"This is incredible, Wilson! How did you create this?" I asked, still in awe.

Wilson's voice was filled with pride. "It took years of research and development. I combined advanced VR technology with detailed environmental simulations to create a truly immersive experience. The goal was to offer a form of escapism that's not just entertaining but also relaxing and mentally stimulating."

As I continued my adventure, collecting artifacts and uncovering secrets, I realized the true potential of Wilson's invention. It wasn't just a game; it was a gateway to another world, a place where you could escape the stresses of everyday life and embark on thrilling adventures.

After what felt like hours, I removed the headset, stepping out of the pod with a sense of wonder. "That was unbelievable, Wilson. You've outdone yourself."

Wilson beamed. "I'm glad you enjoyed it. I think this could offer a lot of people a chance to experience something extraordinary, especially those who might not have the opportunity to travel or explore in real life."

Word of Wilson's Virtual Reality Portal Pod spread quickly. By the end of the week, nearly everyone in Maplewood had heard about the extraordinary device. Neighbors were eager to try it out, and Wilson, always generous with his inventions, organized a series of demonstrations.

The pod became a sensation, attracting people of all ages. Each person who stepped into the pod emerged with a look of awe, their eyes sparkling with excitement. The immersive adventures in tranquil alien landscapes provided a unique blend of relaxation and thrill, making the Virtual Reality Portal Pod a hit.

One evening, as we sat on Wilson's porch watching the stars, he shared more about his motivations. "You know, I've always been fascinated by the idea of exploring other worlds. But I also wanted to create something that could help people relax and escape from their daily routines. The Virtual Reality Portal Pod combines both of those ideas, offering a way to explore and unwind."

His words resonated with me. Wilson's invention was more than just a technological marvel; it was a gift to our community, a way to explore, relax, and find joy in new experiences. By eliminating the barriers to adventure and escapism, Wilson had opened up a world of possibilities for all of us.

As winter approached, the Virtual Reality Portal Pod continued to be a source of excitement and relaxation for Maplewood residents. The immersive experiences offered a welcome respite from the cold, allowing people to escape to sunny alien worlds filled with wonder and discovery.

One day, a local news station visited Maplewood to do a feature on Wilson's invention. As cameras rolled and reporters interviewed residents, Wilson remained humble, focusing on the collective benefits of his creation rather than seeking personal praise.

"It's not about me," he told the reporter. "It's about what we can achieve together. If this invention can bring joy and relaxation to people's lives, then that's all the reward I need."

The news segment aired later that week, showcasing Maplewood's latest technological marvel and highlighting Wilson's role in its creation. People from neighboring communities reached out, eager to experience the Virtual Reality Portal Pod for themselves.

Despite the growing recognition, Wilson remained the same down-to-earth neighbor we all knew and admired. He continued to tinker in his garage, always looking for new ways to solve everyday problems and make life a little better for those around him.

One spring afternoon, as I was tending to my garden, Wilson stopped by with a thoughtful expression on his face. "I've been thinking," he said, "there's so much more we can do with virtual reality technology. What if we could create a network of interconnected pods that allowed people to share their experiences and adventures in real time?"

Intrigued, I listened as Wilson outlined his vision. By linking the pods together, we could create a shared virtual world where people could explore, collaborate, and interact with each other. The possibilities were endless, from collaborative artifact hunts to virtual community gatherings and educational experiences.

"I think it's a fantastic idea," I told him. "And I'm sure our neighbors would be eager to help you test and develop this new system."

Wilson's eyes sparkled with enthusiasm. "That's exactly what I was hoping you'd say. With everyone's input and support, we can take this to the next level."

As the weeks turned into months, Wilson's vision began to take shape. With the help of our neighbors, he developed and tested the interconnected pod system, which quickly proved to be a game-changer. The networked pods allowed us to share our virtual experiences, creating a vibrant, collaborative virtual community.

The results were astounding. Maplewood's residents could now embark on shared adventures, exploring alien worlds together and collecting artifacts as a team. The interconnected system also made it easier for us to organize virtual community events, from educational workshops to social gatherings, bridging the gap between the real and virtual worlds.

Looking back, it's clear that Wilson's Virtual Reality Portal Pod was just the beginning. His invention not only transformed our understanding of virtual reality but also brought us closer together as a community. It inspired us to think creatively about how technology can enrich our lives, foster connections, and open up new realms of possibility.

As I sit on my porch, watching the sun set over the tranquil streets of

Maplewood, I can't help but feel a profound sense of gratitude. Wilson's inventions have changed our neighborhood, but more importantly, they've changed the way we see the world. And for that, we will always be thankful.

The Heart of Steel: Wilson and His Robotic Pet Companion

In the picturesque town of Maplewood, life was a harmonious blend of suburban charm and close-knit community. Among the friendly faces that populated our streets, one stood out more than most—Wilson, our incredibly intelligent neighbor and ingenious inventor. Wilson's home, unassuming from the outside, housed a workshop that was a testament to his creativity and technical prowess. Over the years, he had graced us with numerous inventions that made life easier, greener, and more enjoyable.

One crisp fall morning, as the leaves turned vibrant shades of red and gold, I saw Wilson in his driveway, assembling what looked like a small, lifelike animal. Intrigued, I approached to see what he was working on.

"Good morning, Wilson! What's the latest invention?" I asked, eyeing the remarkably realistic robot.

"Morning! You're just in time to meet my newest creation—the Robotic Pet Companion," Wilson replied, his eyes sparkling with excitement.

"A robotic pet?" I echoed, fascinated by the idea.

Wilson smiled and gestured for me to take a closer look. The robotic pet resembled a small dog, with expressive eyes, a sleek, fur-like covering, and an almost lifelike movement. "Yes, it's designed to provide companionship, especially for those who might not be able to care for a real pet. It's equipped with advanced sensors, emotional responsiveness, and learning capabilities, making it as close to a real pet as possible."

As he spoke, Wilson activated the robotic pet. It came to life with a soft whir, wagging its tail and looking up at me with an almost uncanny curiosity. "Go ahead, interact with it," Wilson encouraged.

I reached out and patted the robot on its head. It responded by leaning into my hand, emitting a contented purr. "This is amazing! It feels so real!" I exclaimed, marveling at the pet's lifelike behavior.

Wilson's grin widened. "That's the idea. It's designed to adapt to its owner's habits and preferences, learning to respond in a way that feels natural and intuitive. It can provide companionship, emotional support, and even help with certain tasks around the house."

The more Wilson explained, the more impressed I became. The Robotic Pet Companion wasn't just a toy; it was a breakthrough in robotics and artificial intelligence. By mimicking the behavior and emotional responsiveness of a real pet, it had the potential to offer comfort and companionship to people who needed it most.

As Wilson demonstrated more of the pet's capabilities, neighbors began to gather, drawn by the sight of the lifelike robot and the promise of a new technological marvel. Wilson explained how the robotic pet could learn its owner's routines, respond to voice commands, and even simulate a range of emotions based on interactions.

The reaction was overwhelmingly positive. People were excited about the idea of a robotic pet, especially those who loved animals but couldn't care for a real one due to allergies, lifestyle, or other constraints. Wilson, always generous with his inventions, offered to let anyone interested take the robotic pet for a test run.

Over the next few weeks, the Robotic Pet Companion became a sensation in Maplewood. Families, seniors, and individuals alike were eager to experience the joy of having a lifelike pet without the responsibilities and challenges that came with a living animal. The robotic pet proved to be an excellent companion, offering comfort, companionship, and even a touch of humor with its playful antics.

One evening, as we sat on Wilson's porch enjoying the crisp autumn air, he shared more about the development process. "Creating the Robotic Pet Companion was a labor of love. I wanted to build something that could genuinely improve people's lives, providing companionship and emotional support. The hardest part was designing the emotional responsiveness and learning algorithms, but seeing the joy it brings makes it all worthwhile."

His words resonated deeply with me. Wilson's invention was more than just a technological marvel; it was a compassionate creation aimed at making life better for those who needed it most. By providing a lifelike companion that could adapt and respond to its owner, Wilson had created something truly special.

As winter approached, the Robotic Pet Companion continued to bring joy and comfort to Maplewood residents. The lifelike pets offered warmth and companionship during the colder months, especially to those who lived alone or faced mobility challenges. The robotic pets quickly became beloved members of many households, providing a sense of connection and emotional support.

One day, a local news station visited Maplewood to do a feature on Wilson's invention. As cameras rolled and reporters interviewed residents, Wilson remained humble, focusing on the collective benefits of his creation rather than seeking personal praise.

"It's not about me," he told the reporter. "It's about what we can achieve together. If this invention can bring joy and comfort to people's lives, then that's all the reward I need."

The news segment aired later that week, showcasing Maplewood's latest technological marvel and highlighting Wilson's role in its creation. People from neighboring communities reached out, eager to experience the Robotic Pet Companion for themselves.

Despite the growing recognition, Wilson remained the same down-to-earth neighbor we all knew and admired. He continued to tinker in his garage, always looking for new ways to solve everyday problems and make life a little better for those around him.

One spring afternoon, as I was tending to my garden, Wilson stopped by with a thoughtful expression on his face. "I've been thinking," he said, "there's so much more we can do with this technology. What if we could create a range of robotic companions, each tailored to different needs and preferences?"

Intrigued, I listened as Wilson outlined his vision. By developing a variety of robotic companions, we could offer support and companionship to a broader audience, from children and families to seniors and individuals with specific needs. The possibilities were endless, from playful and energetic pets to calm and comforting companions.

"I think it's a fantastic idea," I told him. "And I'm sure our neighbors would be eager to help you test and develop these new companions."

Wilson's eyes sparkled with enthusiasm. "That's exactly what I was hoping you'd say. With everyone's input and support, we can take this to the next level."

As the weeks turned into months, Wilson's vision began to take shape. With the help of our neighbors, he developed and tested a range of robotic companions, each designed to provide unique forms of support and companionship. The new companions included robotic cats, birds, and even small mammals, each with its own set of behaviors and capabilities.

The results were astounding. Maplewood's residents could now choose from a variety of lifelike robotic pets, each offering a different type of companionship and emotional support. The new companions quickly became beloved members of many households, providing joy, comfort, and a sense of connection.

Looking back, it's clear that Wilson's Robotic Pet Companion was just the beginning. His invention not only transformed our understanding of robotics and artificial intelligence but also brought us closer together as a community. It inspired us to think creatively about how technology can enrich our lives, foster connections, and open up new realms of possibility.

As I sit on my porch, watching the sun set over the tranquil streets of Maplewood, I can't help but feel a profound sense of gratitude. Wilson's inventions have changed our neighborhood, but more importantly, they've changed the way we see the world. And for that, we will always be thankful.

The Water Revolution: Wilson and His Robotic Rainwater Collection Hydroponic Garden

In the picturesque town of Maplewood, where community and innovation walked hand in hand, there lived an inventor named Wilson. Wilson's unassuming home housed a workshop where creativity and technology intertwined, producing inventions that continually enhanced our lives. From solar-powered lawn mowers to lifelike robotic pets, Wilson's innovations had made Maplewood a model of modern living.

One bright spring morning, as the smell of fresh rain lingered in the air, I noticed Wilson working on something new in his driveway. The contraption looked like a futuristic garden system, complete with sleek tubes, LED lights, and an array of sensors. Intrigued, I walked over to see what Wilson was up to.

"Good morning, Wilson! What's the latest invention?" I asked, eyeing the complex setup with curiosity.

"Morning! You're just in time to see my newest creation—the Robotic Rainwater Collection Hydroponic Garden," Wilson replied, his face lighting up with excitement.

"A hydroponic garden?" I echoed, fascinated by the idea.

Wilson smiled and motioned for me to take a closer look. "Yes, it's a garden system designed to collect rainwater and use hydroponics and LED lighting to grow vegetables and herbs efficiently. It's ideal for urban settings where space is limited, and it's fully automated to ensure optimal growth conditions."

As he spoke, Wilson demonstrated how the system worked. Rainwater was collected in a reservoir, filtered, and then circulated through the hydroponic setup, where plants grew in nutrient-rich water instead of soil. LED lights provided the necessary spectrum for photosynthesis, ensuring healthy plant growth regardless of the weather outside.

"The best part," Wilson explained, "is that the entire system is robotic. It monitors and adjusts water levels, nutrient concentration, and light exposure to maintain the perfect growing conditions. You can grow fresh produce year-round with minimal effort."

I was amazed by the simplicity and efficiency of the design. "That's incredible, Wilson! How did you come up with this?"

Wilson's eyes twinkled with enthusiasm. "I've always been passionate about sustainable living and urban agriculture. With more people living in cities and space becoming a premium, I wanted to create a system that allows anyone to grow their own food, no matter how small their living space. By using rainwater and hydroponics, we can conserve resources and reduce our environmental footprint."

As Wilson continued to explain the benefits of his invention, neighbors began to gather, drawn by the sight of the futuristic garden and the promise of fresh, home-grown produce. Wilson showed how the system could be easily installed on balconies, rooftops, or even indoors, making it accessible to everyone.

The reaction was overwhelmingly positive. People were excited about the idea of growing their own vegetables and herbs, especially in an environmentally friendly way. Wilson, always generous with his inventions, offered to set up a few pilot systems for interested neighbors.

Over the next few weeks, Wilson's Robotic Rainwater Collection Hydroponic Garden became a sensation in Maplewood. Families, seniors, and individuals alike were eager to try it out, and the pilot systems quickly proved their worth. Fresh produce was abundant, and the ease of use made the system a hit with everyone.

One evening, as we sat on Wilson's porch enjoying the mild spring air, he shared more about the development process. "Creating the hydroponic garden was challenging but rewarding. I had to design a system that was not only efficient but also user-friendly and adaptable to different environments. Seeing how much people are enjoying it makes all the hard work worthwhile."

His words resonated deeply with me. Wilson's invention was more than just a technological marvel; it was a step towards sustainable living and self-sufficiency. By providing an easy and efficient way to grow fresh produce, Wilson had created something truly impactful.

As summer approached, the Robotic Rainwater Collection Hydroponic Garden continued to flourish. The fresh vegetables and herbs added a new dimension to our meals, and the satisfaction of growing our own food brought a sense of accomplishment and connection to nature.

One day, a local news station visited Maplewood to do a feature on Wilson's invention. As cameras rolled and reporters interviewed residents, Wilson remained humble, focusing on the collective benefits of his creation rather than seeking personal praise.

"It's not about me," he told the reporter. "It's about what we can achieve together. If this invention can help people grow their own food and live more sustainably, then that's all the reward I need."

The news segment aired later that week, showcasing Maplewood's latest technological marvel and highlighting Wilson's role in its creation. People from neighboring communities reached out, eager to experience the hydroponic garden for themselves.

Despite the growing recognition, Wilson remained the same down-to-earth neighbor we all knew and admired. He continued to tinker in his garage, always looking for new ways to solve everyday problems and make life a little better for those around him.

One fall afternoon, as I was harvesting basil from my hydroponic garden, Wilson stopped by with a thoughtful expression on his face. "I've been thinking," he said, "there's so much more we can do with this technology. What if we could create a community garden using these systems, allowing people to share resources and produce?"

Intrigued, I listened as Wilson outlined his vision. By creating a network of interconnected hydroponic systems, we could establish a community garden where people could grow and share their produce. The possibilities were endless, from collaborative gardening projects to educational workshops on sustainable living.

"I think it's a fantastic idea," I told him. "And I'm sure our neighbors would be eager to help you test and develop this community garden."

Wilson's eyes sparkled with enthusiasm. "That's exactly what I was hoping you'd say. With everyone's input and support, we can take this to the next level."

As the weeks turned into months, Wilson's vision began to take shape. With the help of our neighbors, he developed and tested a network of interconnected hydroponic systems, which quickly proved to be a game-changer. The community garden brought us closer together, fostering a sense of collaboration and shared purpose.

The results were astounding. Maplewood's residents could now grow a wide variety of vegetables and herbs, pooling their resources and knowledge to create a thriving garden. The community garden also became a focal point for social gatherings and educational events, promoting sustainable living and self-sufficiency.

Looking back, it's clear that Wilson's Robotic Rainwater Collection Hydroponic Garden was just the beginning. His invention not only transformed our understanding of urban agriculture but also brought us closer together as a community. It inspired us to think creatively about how technology can enrich our lives, foster connections, and open up new realms of possibility.

As I sit on my porch, watching the sun set over the lush green of our community garden, I can't help but feel a profound sense of gratitude. Wilson's inventions have changed our neighborhood, but more importantly, they've changed the way we see the world. And for that, we will always be thankful.

A Cleaner Tomorrow: Wilson and His Smart Trash Compactor

In the quaint and ever-evolving town of Maplewood, where innovation met community spirit, Wilson was a local hero. Renowned for his ingenious inventions that seamlessly integrated technology into daily life, Wilson had transformed our town into a model of modern living. From automated lawn mowers to lifelike robotic pets, his creations had simplified our lives and enriched our experiences.

One crisp autumn morning, I noticed Wilson busy in his garage, tinkering with what looked like a sleek, futuristic trash bin. Curious as always, I wandered over to see what new marvel he was working on.

"Good morning, Wilson! What's the latest invention?" I asked, peering at the intriguing device.

"Morning! You're just in time to see my newest creation—the Smart Trash Compactor," Wilson replied, his eyes gleaming with excitement.

"A smart trash compactor?" I echoed, intrigued by the concept.

Wilson smiled and gestured for me to take a closer look. "Yes, it's a compacting trash bin equipped with sensors that monitor waste levels. It notifies homeowners when it needs emptying, significantly reducing the number of trips to the curb."

As he spoke, Wilson demonstrated how the system worked. The trash compactor, a sleek, modern design, was more than just a bin. It featured advanced sensors that detected waste levels and a compaction mechanism that significantly reduced the volume of trash. An integrated app allowed users to receive notifications and monitor the bin's status in real-time.

"The best part," Wilson explained, "is that the compactor not only reduces the volume of trash but also ensures that you only take it out when it's full. It's efficient, environmentally friendly, and ideal for busy households."

I was impressed by the simplicity and practicality of the design. "That's incredible, Wilson! How did you come up with this?"

Wilson's face lit up with enthusiasm. "I've always been passionate about sustainability and efficient living. The idea came to me after seeing how often people in our community were taking out half-full trash bags. I wanted to create a solution that would save time and reduce waste, both in terms of volume and unnecessary plastic bags."

As Wilson continued to explain the benefits of his invention, neighbors began to gather, drawn by the sight of the sleek trash compactor and the promise of a more efficient waste management solution. Wilson showed how the compactor's sensors worked, triggering notifications when the bin was full and ready to be emptied.

The reaction was overwhelmingly positive. People were excited about the idea of a smart trash compactor, especially those with large families or busy schedules. Wilson, always generous with his inventions, offered to set up a few pilot units for interested neighbors.

Over the next few weeks, Wilson's Smart Trash Compactor became a sensation in Maplewood. Families, seniors, and individuals alike were eager to try it out, and the pilot units quickly proved their worth. Trash collection became more efficient, and the reduction in trips to the curb was a welcome change for everyone.

One evening, as we sat on Wilson's porch enjoying the cool autumn air, he shared more about the development process. "Creating the smart trash compactor was a challenge, but seeing how much people appreciate it makes all the hard work worthwhile. The biggest hurdle was designing the sensors to be both accurate and durable, but I'm happy with how it turned out."

His words resonated deeply with me. Wilson's invention was more than just a technological marvel; it was a practical solution to a common problem, designed to make life easier and more sustainable. By providing a smart and efficient way to manage household waste, Wilson had created something truly impactful.

As winter approached, the Smart Trash Compactor continued to make life easier for Maplewood residents. The convenience of receiving notifications and the reduced number of trips to the curb made the cold months more manageable. The compactors quickly became indispensable household items, appreciated for their practicality and environmental benefits.

One day, a local news station visited Maplewood to do a feature on Wilson's invention. As cameras rolled and reporters interviewed residents, Wilson remained humble, focusing on the collective benefits of his creation rather than seeking personal praise.

"It's not about me," he told the reporter. "It's about what we can achieve together. If this invention can make life easier and more sustainable for people, then that's all the reward I need."

The news segment aired later that week, showcasing Maplewood's latest technological marvel and highlighting Wilson's role in its creation. People from neighboring communities reached out, eager to experience the Smart Trash Compactor for themselves.

Despite the growing recognition, Wilson remained the same down-to-earth neighbor we all knew and admired. He continued to tinker in his garage, always looking for new ways to solve everyday problems and make life a little better for those around him.

One spring afternoon, as I was taking out my now much lighter trash, Wilson stopped by with a thoughtful expression on his face. "I've been thinking," he said, "there's so much more we can do with smart home technology. What if we could integrate the trash compactor with other systems, like recycling and composting, to create a fully automated waste management solution?"

Intrigued, I listened as Wilson outlined his vision. By creating an integrated system that managed all types of waste, from trash to recycling to composting, we could significantly reduce our environmental footprint and make waste management even more efficient.

"I think it's a fantastic idea," I told him. "And I'm sure our neighbors would be eager to help you test and develop this integrated system."

Wilson's eyes sparkled with enthusiasm. "That's exactly what I was hoping you'd say. With everyone's input and support, we can take this to the next level."

As the weeks turned into months, Wilson's vision began to take shape. With the help of our neighbors, he developed and tested a fully integrated waste management system. The new system included smart recycling bins and composters, each equipped with sensors and connected to a central app for seamless management.

The results were astounding. Maplewood's residents could now manage all their waste efficiently, receiving notifications and updates through a single app. The integrated system not only reduced waste but also encouraged more sustainable living practices, like composting and proper recycling.

Looking back, it's clear that Wilson's Smart Trash Compactor was just the beginning. His invention not only transformed our understanding of waste management but also brought us closer together as a community. It inspired us to think creatively about how technology can enrich our lives, foster connections, and open up new realms of possibility.

As I sit on my porch, watching the sun set over the clean, green streets of Maplewood, I can't help but feel a profound sense of gratitude. Wilson's inventions have changed our neighborhood, but more importantly, they've changed the way we see the world. And for that, we will always be thankful.

The Future of Safety: Wilson and His Augmented Reality Home Security System

In the charming town of Maplewood, innovation was part of everyday life. This was largely thanks to our incredibly intelligent neighbor, Wilson. His home, a modest house with a sprawling workshop in the back, was a birthplace of modern marvels that continuously improved our lives. From solar-powered devices to smart home solutions, Wilson's inventions made Maplewood a beacon of progressive living.

One crisp autumn morning, as the leaves painted the town in hues of orange and gold, I saw Wilson working intently on something new in his garage. This time, it wasn't a device but rather an array of small cameras and sleek glasses spread across his workbench. Curiosity piqued, I decided to find out what Wilson was up to.

"Good morning, Wilson! What's the latest invention?" I asked, stepping into his workshop.

"Morning! You're just in time to see my newest creation—the Augmented Reality Home Security System," Wilson replied, his eyes gleaming with excitement.

"Augmented reality for home security?" I echoed, intrigued by the concept.

Wilson smiled and gestured for me to take a closer look at the setup. "Yes, it's a system that overlays real-time security alerts and surveillance footage onto smart glasses or a mobile app. This way, homeowners can see what's happening around their property in real-time, enhancing their security awareness."

As he spoke, Wilson demonstrated how the system worked. Tiny, unobtrusive cameras were positioned around the house, feeding live footage to a central hub. This footage was then transmitted to smart glasses or a mobile app, which overlaid the video onto the user's field of view using augmented reality (AR) technology.

"The best part," Wilson explained, "is that it provides an immersive experience, making it feel like you're looking through a window rather than at a screen. You get real-time alerts for any suspicious activity, and you can view the footage from anywhere, whether you're at home or away."

I was amazed by the practicality and innovation of the design. "That's incredible, Wilson! How did you come up with this?"

Wilson's face lit up with enthusiasm. "I've always been passionate about integrating technology to enhance everyday life. Home security is a critical concern for many people, and I wanted to create a system that not only provides robust security but also integrates seamlessly with modern lifestyles. By using AR, we can give homeowners a powerful tool to monitor their property in real-time."

As Wilson continued to explain the benefits of his invention, neighbors began to gather, drawn by the sight of the sleek cameras and the promise of a new level of home security. Wilson showed how the smart glasses worked, allowing users to see real-time surveillance footage and alerts superimposed onto their surroundings.

The reaction was overwhelmingly positive. People were excited about the idea of an augmented reality home security system, especially those who valued both safety and cutting-edge technology. Wilson, always generous with his inventions, offered to set up a few pilot systems for interested neighbors.

Over the next few weeks, Wilson's Augmented Reality Home Security System became a sensation in Maplewood. Families, seniors, and tech enthusiasts alike were eager to try it out, and the pilot systems quickly proved their worth. Homeowners felt more secure and connected, knowing they could monitor their property in real-time with just a glance.

One evening, as we sat on Wilson's porch enjoying the crisp autumn air, he shared more about the development process. "Creating the AR security system was challenging but rewarding. The hardest part was ensuring the real-time overlay was seamless and intuitive. But seeing how much peace of mind it brings to people makes it all worthwhile."

His words resonated deeply with me. Wilson's invention was more than just a technological marvel; it was a practical solution to a common concern, designed to make life safer and more secure. By providing an immersive and real-time way to monitor one's home, Wilson had created something truly impactful.

As winter approached, the Augmented Reality Home Security System continued to enhance the safety of Maplewood residents. The convenience of receiving real-time alerts and viewing live footage through AR made the cold months more bearable, knowing that our homes were well-protected. The AR systems quickly became indispensable, appreciated for their practicality and advanced technology.

One day, a local news station visited Maplewood to do a feature on Wilson's invention. As cameras rolled and reporters interviewed residents, Wilson remained humble, focusing on the collective benefits of his creation rather than seeking personal praise.

"It's not about me," he told the reporter. "It's about what we can achieve together. If this invention can enhance home security and give people peace of mind, then that's all the reward I need."

The news segment aired later that week, showcasing Maplewood's latest technological marvel and highlighting Wilson's role in its creation. People from neighboring communities reached out, eager to experience the Augmented Reality Home Security System for themselves.

Despite the growing recognition, Wilson remained the same down-to-earth neighbor we all knew and admired. He continued to tinker in his garage, always looking for new ways to solve everyday problems and make life a little better for those around him.

One spring afternoon, as I was checking the AR security footage of my front yard, Wilson stopped by with a thoughtful expression on his face. "I've been thinking," he said, "there's so much more we can do with AR technology. What if we could integrate it with other home systems, like lighting and climate control, to create a fully immersive smart home experience?"

Intrigued, I listened as Wilson outlined his vision. By creating an integrated AR system that managed not only security but also other home functions, we could significantly enhance the convenience and efficiency of our living spaces.

"I think it's a fantastic idea," I told him. "And I'm sure our neighbors would be eager to help you test and develop this integrated system."

Wilson's eyes sparkled with enthusiasm. "That's exactly what I was hoping you'd say. With everyone's input and support, we can take this to the next level."

As the weeks turned into months, Wilson's vision began to take shape. With the help of our neighbors, he developed and tested a fully integrated AR home system. The new system included smart lighting, climate control, and even entertainment options, all accessible through the same AR interface.

The results were astounding. Maplewood's residents could now control their entire home environment through AR, receiving real-time updates and managing various functions with ease. The integrated system not only enhanced security but also made everyday tasks more convenient and efficient.

Looking back, it's clear that Wilson's Augmented Reality Home Security System was just the beginning. His invention not only transformed our understanding of home security but also brought us closer together as a community. It inspired us to think creatively about how technology can enrich our lives, foster connections, and open up new realms of possibility.

As I sit on my porch, watching the sun set over the secure and connected homes of Maplewood, I can't help but feel a profound sense of gratitude. Wilson's inventions have changed our neighborhood, but more importantly, they've changed the way we see the world. And for that, we will always be thankful.

Wilson's Defense: The Biometric Fence with Laser Cannons

In the picturesque town of Maplewood, where innovation seamlessly blended with everyday life, Wilson was a local legend. His modest home and sprawling workshop were the epicenters of technological breakthroughs that continually improved our community. From smart lawn mowers to augmented reality home security systems, Wilson's inventions had made Maplewood a beacon of modern living.

One sunny afternoon, as I strolled past Wilson's house, I noticed an elaborate setup in his front yard. A sleek, high-tech fence with glinting metal panels and what looked like small turret-like structures piqued my curiosity. I couldn't resist the urge to find out what Wilson was working on this time.

"Good afternoon, Wilson! What's the latest invention?" I called out, approaching his workshop.

"Afternoon! You're just in time to see my newest creation—the Biometric Fence with Laser Cannons," Wilson replied, his eyes sparkling with excitement.

"A biometric fence with laser cannons?" I echoed, both intrigued and slightly wary.

Wilson chuckled at my reaction and gestured for me to come closer. "Yes, it's a high-security fence equipped with biometric sensors and laser cannons. It recognizes authorized individuals, adjusts access permissions, and monitors the perimeter for any security breaches."

As he spoke, Wilson demonstrated how the system worked. The fence was embedded with advanced biometric sensors that could identify individuals through fingerprints, facial recognition, and even retinal scans. Once an authorized individual was recognized, the system would grant access, allowing the fence panels to retract smoothly.

"The laser cannons," Wilson continued, pointing to the turret-like structures, "are for perimeter security. They're equipped with non-lethal lasers that can temporarily disable intruders or alert authorities in case of a breach."

I was amazed by the sophistication and practicality of the design. "That's incredible, Wilson! How did you come up with this?"

Wilson's face lit up with enthusiasm. "I've always been passionate about security and cutting-edge technology. The idea came to me after hearing about several break-ins in our neighboring towns. I wanted to create a solution that provides robust security without being overly intrusive or dangerous."

As Wilson continued to explain the benefits of his invention, neighbors began to gather, drawn by the sight of the futuristic fence and the promise of enhanced security. Wilson showed how the biometric sensors worked, demonstrating how the fence granted access to authorized individuals while maintaining a secure perimeter.

The reaction was overwhelmingly positive. People were excited about the idea of a high-security fence, especially those who valued both safety and technological innovation. Wilson, always generous with his inventions, offered to set up a few pilot systems for interested neighbors.

Over the next few weeks, Wilson's Biometric Fence with Laser Cannons became a sensation in Maplewood. Families, businesses, and tech enthusiasts alike were eager to try it out, and the pilot systems quickly proved their worth. Homeowners felt more secure, knowing that their properties were protected by state-of-the-art technology.

One evening, as we sat on Wilson's porch enjoying the mild spring air, he shared more about the development process. "Creating the biometric fence was challenging but rewarding. The hardest part was ensuring the biometric sensors were accurate and reliable under various conditions. But seeing how much peace of mind it brings to people makes it all worthwhile."

His words resonated deeply with me. Wilson's invention was more than just a technological marvel; it was a practical solution to a common concern, designed to make life safer and more secure. By providing a high-tech and non-lethal way to protect properties, Wilson had created something truly impactful.

As summer approached, the Biometric Fence with Laser Cannons continued to enhance the security of Maplewood residents. The convenience of biometric access and the added layer of laser protection made the warm months more enjoyable, knowing that our homes and businesses were well-protected. The fences quickly became indispensable, appreciated for their practicality and advanced technology.

One day, a local news station visited Maplewood to do a feature on Wilson's invention. As cameras rolled and reporters interviewed residents, Wilson remained humble, focusing on the collective benefits of his creation rather than seeking personal praise.

"It's not about me," he told the reporter. "It's about what we can achieve together. If this invention can enhance security and give people peace of mind, then that's all the reward I need."

The news segment aired later that week, showcasing Maplewood's latest technological marvel and highlighting Wilson's role in its creation. People from neighboring communities reached out, eager to experience the Biometric Fence with Laser Cannons for themselves.

Despite the growing recognition, Wilson remained the same down-to-earth neighbor we all knew and admired. He continued to tinker in his garage, always looking for new ways to solve everyday problems and make life a little better for those around him.

One autumn afternoon, as I was inspecting the biometric fence surrounding my property, Wilson stopped by with a thoughtful expression on his face. "I've been thinking," he said, "there's so much more we can do with this technology. What if we could integrate it with other smart home systems to create a fully comprehensive security solution?"

Intrigued, I listened as Wilson outlined his vision. By creating an integrated system that managed not only the fence but also other security functions, like surveillance, lighting, and alarm systems, we could significantly enhance the overall security of our homes.

"I think it's a fantastic idea," I told him. "And I'm sure our neighbors would be eager to help you test and develop this integrated system."

Wilson's eyes sparkled with enthusiasm. "That's exactly what I was hoping you'd say. With everyone's input and support, we can take this to the next level."

As the weeks turned into months, Wilson's vision began to take shape. With the help of our neighbors, he developed and tested a fully integrated home security system. The new system included smart surveillance cameras, automated lighting, and advanced alarm systems, all connected through a central hub and accessible via a mobile app.

The results were astounding. Maplewood's residents could now manage their entire home security system from one platform, receiving real-time updates and alerts. The integrated system not only enhanced security but also made everyday tasks more convenient and efficient.

Looking back, it's clear that Wilson's Biometric Fence with Laser Cannons was just the beginning. His invention not only transformed our understanding of home security but also brought us closer together as a community. It inspired us to think creatively about how technology can enrich our lives, foster connections, and open up new realms of possibility.

As I sit on my porch, watching the sun set over the secure and connected homes of Maplewood, I can't help but feel a profound sense of gratitude. Wilson's inventions have changed our neighborhood, but more importantly, they've changed the way we see the world. And for that, we will always be thankful.

Epilogue: A Future of Innovation and Security

Wilson's Biometric Fence with Laser Cannons and the subsequent integrated security system became benchmarks in home security technology. They not only enhanced the safety of Maplewood but also set a precedent for communities worldwide. As word of Wilson's innovations spread, his expertise was sought far and wide, inspiring a new wave of security solutions that combined advanced technology with practical, everyday applications.

Through his relentless pursuit of innovation and his unwavering commitment to improving the lives of those around him, Wilson had not only fortified the physical boundaries of our homes but also strengthened the bonds within our community. His legacy of creativity, generosity, and vision for a safer, smarter world continues to inspire us all.

www.ingramcontent.com/pod-product-compliance
Lightning Source LLC
La Vergne TN
LVHW051242050326
832903LV00028B/2533